BEAU BRUMMELL

Ron Hutchinson

BEAU BRUMMELL

AN ELEGANT MADNESS

OBERON BOOKS
LONDON

WWW.OBERONBOOKS.COM

First published in 2001 by Oberon Books Ltd
521 Caledonian Road, London N7 9RH
Tel: +44 (0) 20 7607 3637 / Fax: +44 (0) 20 7607 3629
e-mail: info@oberonbooks.com
www.oberonbooks.com

A catalogue record for this book is available from the British
Library.

PB ISBN: 9781840022315
E ISBN: 9781786821577

Cover photography by Emily Hyland
Cover design by Richard Mott

Printed and bound by Marston Book Services, Didcot.
eBook conversion by CPI Group (UK) Ltd, Croydon, CR0 4YY.

Visit www.oberonbooks.com to read more about all our books
and to buy them. You will also find features, author interviews and
news of any author events, and you can sign up for e-newsletters
so that you're always first to hear about our new releases.

Characters

BEAU BRUMMELL

AUSTIN

Beau Brummell was first performed at the Theatre Royal Bath on 27 February 2001, with the following cast:

BEAU BRUMMELL, Peter Bowles

AUSTIN, Richard McCabe

Director, Caroline Hunt

Designer, Ashley Martin-Davis

Lighting Designer, Paul Pyant

Sound Designer, Gina Hills

Costume Supervisor, Alistair McArthur

This production opened at Jermyn Street Theatre, London on 13 February 2017 and was presented by European Arts Company with the following cast:

BEAU BRUMMELL, Sean Brosnan

AUSTIN, Richard Latham

Director, Peter Craze

Producer, John O'Connor

Designer, Helen Coyston

Lighting Designer, Duncan Hands

Stage Manager, Lucy Myers

Act One

A phantasmagoria of eighteenth and early nineteenth costumes piled several feet high – brocades and silks and velvets; hats spilling out of hat boxes; wigs on wig stands; boots; waistcoats of every color. It's as if someone has tipped out the contents of several wardrobes and scattered them around. There's also a large, marble bust of Homer.

They, and oversize framed political cartoons by Gillray and Cruickshank, frame a squalid chamber in a madhouse in Calais in the winter of 1819. Despite the cold a man is sitting in an enamel bath in the middle of the room. He's BEAU BRUMMELL, aged fifty. He is holding a cut throat razor at his throat.

There's nothing effeminate about Brummell – he couldn't have kept his position in the masculine world of the Regency swells if there had been. He's still handsome, despite the privations he's enduring in exile; his manner still retains its graciousness, although he suffers from alarming mood swings and gives in without warning to violent despair.

The first thing we hear is his scream, as he tries to summons up the courage to slash.

His valet, AUSTIN, is trying to persuade him to drop the razor. Austin is younger than Brummell, with a quick intelligence and given to as sudden shifts in mood as his master. He's also carrying numerous chips on his shoulder which from time to time give him a sullen, brooding quality.

AUSTIN: Put it down.

> *BRUMMELL screams again, tries to nerve himself to cut his throat.*
>
> Give me the razor.
>
> *Another scream, another halfhearted attempt.*
>
> The Duke of Norfolk's coming any minute.
>
> *BRUMMELL hesitates.*

BRUMMELL: Norfolk?

AUSTIN: How would it look, you in the bath with your throat cut?

BRUMMELL: He's in Calais?

AUSTIN: On his way here, this minute, yes.

AUSTIN looks at the door, as if he's heard something –

Is that him?

BRUMMELL: Who?

AUSTIN: Norfolk. At the door, now.

(Towards the door.)

Your Grace?

BRUMMELL: I'm not at home to anyone today.

AUSTIN: Not even the Duke of Norfolk?

BRUMMELL: Norfolk or not, I can't stand another day here.

AUSTIN: Thank God we're going back, then. It's been – I mean, it's not been – has it? Look at you. Back to England, not half.

BRUMMELL: Where, pray, would I live? London? A cess pit. Brighton? A whore house. Bath? A piss pot.

AUSTIN: I like Bath, me.

BRUMMELL: You would. It's the most vicious, corrupt town in Europe.

AUSTIN: There's Bristol.

BRUMMELL: Uh.

AUSTIN: Norwich?

BRUMMELL: Uh.

AUSTIN: Swindon?

BRUMMELL: Uh.

AUSTIN: Manchester?

BRUMMELL: *(Shudder.)* The North?

AUSTIN: Might as well freeze to death there as here.

BRUMMELL: The 10th Light Dragoons were ordered to Manchester to put down some civil unrest when I was their Captain. I went to the Prince and told him I would have to resign my commission, I couldn't possibly be seen somewhere so unfashionable.

AUSTIN carefully positions himself to make a grab for the razor.

I shan't go back to England.

The Englishman is essentially frivolous. He is surrounded on all sides by a body of water which protects him from the real world; the bloodlust into which Europe is plunged from time to time is something which, if he is to indulge himself in, he does so voluntarily.

He's favored by nature, too. He has no hurricanoes to fear; no tigers, no wolves or scorpions. Of all men he is most likely to die in his bed; how can such a man feel tragedy? Marriage is the nearest he'll come to experiencing it. It would be as absurd for him to go through life taking things seriously as for a Russian serf to see the funny side of things.

The Englishman, sir, in his own most telling phrase, *mustn't grumble* because, when you get down to it, he has nothing to grumble at; I should find that dull, after France.

AUSTIN: The razor?

BRUMMELL: Besides, here I require no carriage, no establishment, no underfootmen or second butler eating his head off at my expense – only you.

AUSTIN: Speaking of wages –

BRUMMELL: *(Ignoring it.)* The noise in London – the clatter of wheels and hooves night and day; the clamor of Brighton; the *frenzy* of Bath – all those card games and balls and masques and views and exhibitions and subscription concerts – compare that to here –

A bell chimes quietly outside –

Listen –

Who would cast off that pastoral tintinnabulation for anything that England has to offer?

AUSTIN grabs for the razor but BRUMMELL pulls it out of his reach. It's at his throat again.

One quick slash, one moment of stupefaction – then oblivion –

AUSTIN keeps his eye on the razor, talking rapidly.

AUSTIN: There's nowhere like Bath. If I had the money I'd set myself up in the sedan chair business. I'd get hold of six of the biggest farm laborers I could find – they're big sods in Somerset – buy a couple of chairs and make a killing.

BRUMMELL: I've seen the last of Albion and it of me.

AUSTIN: Six laborers, a halfpenny a day – hire of chair sixpence –

BRUMMELL: I should never be allowed peace, there. I am too much the Monument, I should be sought out as if I were some hippopotamus or raree – *There is Beau Brummell*, they would say, *no visit to England is complete without a sight of the Tower or of him.*

AUSTIN: You get some fat alderman who doesn't want to pay up – tip him out of the chair bollock naked in the High Street – the other's'd get the message.

BRUMMELL: I should be an *attraction*. Me, whose entire life has been dedicated to the belief that a true gentleman is one who can walk down the street without being remarked on.

AUSTIN grabs the razor, throws it out of BRUMMELL's reach onto a tray of shaving items. AUSTIN's shaking with the release from tension.

AUSTIN: This can't go on.

BRUMMELL: Oh but it can, there's the horror of it.

He looks at himself in the bath –

Do hurry up. I can't receive the premier peer of England *in naturabilis*. What a disgusting thing the naked body is.

The knee. What was God thinking of when he designed something so ugly?

Towel.

AUSTIN holds up a large towel and wraps BRUMMELL in it, patting him dry.

Do you think we go unclothed to Heaven? If so, I can't conceive of wanting to go there, on aesthetic grounds; a fat duchess with all her clothes removed is, I should hazard, one of the most dreadful sights in nature, run second only by her husband.

AUSTIN: I never give it a thought.

He hands BRUMMELL a sheet of paper.

Sign here.

BRUMMELL takes the pen he hands him, dips it into the ink pot and signs. AUSTIN whips the paper away quickly.

BRUMMELL: Your boot may have a soul but does your hat? Your drawers? The Bible is silent but if it's not so there we shall be, for all eternity, with our varicose veins and the scars of old boils.

(Shudders.)

Hideous.

AUSTIN: That's your trouble, too much thinking. Hour after hour, day after day, wearing yourself out with it. I think as little as I can and I'm the happier for it.

BRUMMELL: Every man carries his idea of Paradise inside him, even a valet.

AUSTIN: Bath in the Season. The carriages. The serving girls. All those fat buggers who think they've got something wrong with them needing to be carried to the Pump Room every morning, to the physician to be cupped in the afternoon and then off to the concert at night. The *pickings*. That's Paradise.

BRUMMELL: What does Norfolk want?

AUSTIN: What do they all want? Gloucester, Bedford, Northumberland, all the rest of them – you're Beau Brummell.

'Is it true, Mr. Brummell, that you take two hours each morning scrubbing yourself with a pigs-bristle brush?'.

'Did you once discard twenty-three stocks because you couldn't get them tied right?'

'Do you really have one glovemaker do the fingers and the other the thumbs?'

BRUMMELL: Style is in the details.

Clothes.

AUSTIN indicates a screen on which are draped BRUMMEL's underwear, a flowered chintz dressing gown and a velvet night cap with gold tassels. BRUMMELL shivers as he starts to dress, covered by the towel.

Are you trying to kill me? The fire's gone out.

AUSTIN: You will have your bath. It took all the wood to warm the water.

BRUMMELL: Buy more.

AUSTIN: With what?

BRUMMELL: Chop up the furniture, then.

AUSTIN: We did that.

BRUMMELL: Perhaps it's just as well. The Prince comes to Calais today. He'll take one look around here and realize to what depths of humiliation I've been reduced. *'Brummell!'* he'll say *'Beau!'*. Tears will spring to his eyes, he'll fall on my neck and beg my forgiveness.

AUSTIN: And I'll get paid?

BRUMMELL: His route takes him past that window. He'll look up and see me. He'll call for the carriage to be stopped, race up the stairs, throw open the door –

AUSTIN: Isn't he too fat to be racing up anything?

BRUMMELL: There's a good heart there, a large Hanoverian heart.

AUSTIN: And a big backside.

BRUMMELL: True, no one over twenty stone looks their best in pink knee breeches but –

AUSTIN: So we are going back to England, then?

BRUMMELL: Why is he here in France, if not for a reconciliation?

AUSTIN: Peace treaties, seeing other monarchs?

BRUMMELL: Oh yes, yes – those are his official duties – but the Prince's –

AUSTIN: King's –

BRUMMELL: – most prized possession was always his feeling. He is a passionate man. The English like him for that, they're a passionate people, that's what makes them so hard to rule.

(Shudders.)

This linen is filthy.

AUSTIN: It's all you've got left.

(Trying to keep it straight.)

So you do want to go back?

BRUMMELL: *(Ignoring it.)* When was it washed?

AUSTIN: I'm a valet, not a laundress.

BRUMMELL: Valet? *Valet?* My grandfather was a valet. He'd have shot himself rather than hand his master linen like this.

AUSTIN: Suit yourself.

After all this time, he'll still remember you, will he?

BRUMMELL: Why should he not remember me?

AUSTIN: Well he might *remember* you – there's that arsehole, he might say, who called me a fat fucker in front of everybody.

BRUMMELL: I did not call him a fat fucker and while in my employment have a care for your language.

AUSTIN: Employment?

(Brandishes the notebook.)

I haven't been paid in twelve months. Here.

He hands him another sheet of paper which BRUMMELL signs without looking at.

BRUMMELL: There was a misunderstanding between us, that's all.

BRUMMELL closes his eyes. There's a sound of music, voices, laughter in a distant, crowded room. The lighting state changes.

BRUMMELL: *(Haunted by memory.)* The Argyle Rooms.

For some time I have felt a growing coolness from the Prince.

Music. Glittering gowns. Dancing. Chatter. Everyone of importance in the most important, the most brilliant city in the world. Wits. Politicians. Royalty. Art. Poetry.

In the reflection of a mirror I see the Prince of Wales enter. I know he sees me, the glass tells me that much. With deliberation, he turns his back to me.

He's the size of a small coach. Be-wigged, covered in ribbons and bows and medals and gold braid and epaulets. He takes Lord Alvanley by the elbow. His face is hideous with powder, sweat, rouge, chalk. The eyes are those of a frightened pig, the mouth weak, sensuous, blubbery. He waves his fat hands as he speaks, covered with rings, fingers white as slugs.

He still ignores me. Tee-hees and ha-has at something Alvanley says. His eyes never still, jumping from one thing to the next, like his conversation.

AUSTIN: *(Apprehensive.)* That's enough –

BRUMMELL: My stomach rebels. My head spins. I'm being cut – cut by this grotesque fool, this Royal laughing stock.

AUSTIN: You promised – –

BRUMMELL: I'd given him my friendship, tried to teach him everything I know of Style and Wit –

AUSTIN: It doesn't do you any good –

BRUMMELL: Heads are turned towards us. Whispering. Laughter. Everyone knows. The Prince is cutting Brummell.

I clear my throat. I say *'Who's your fat friend, Alvanley?'* and it's over, all of it, over.

The music ends, the lighting state changes back.

(Weakly, pleading.)

There was no malice there, no intent to draw blood – just the faintest pinprick –

'Who's your fat friend?'

It was my enemies who poisoned him against me and drove me into exile.

AUSTIN: Not the fact you spent all your money on cards?

BRUMMELL: I played a hand of vingt-et-un once in a while, yes.

AUSTIN: For fifty thousand pounds a hand.

BRUMMELL: Now and again play got a little hot, yes.

AUSTIN: You lost the lot.

BRUMMELL: You're a valet, you wouldn't understand the importance of losing well.

AUSTIN: Was it worth it?

BRUMMELL: There is no greater tribute to the quality of English society than the number of Englishmen who will throw all their fortune away on the turn of a card or the toss of a dice.

AUSTIN: Even though it beggars their family and everyone they owe money too?

BRUMMELL: That is a small price to pay for a display of character.

AUSTIN: So you've been happy here, have you? Freezing to death?

BRUMMELL looks around at his squalid lodgings.

BRUMMELL: Give me the razor.

AUSTIN: No.

BRUMMELL: Then you cut my throat.

(Despairing.)

Dear God, what is the point of existence if it is not to be seen, not to be received, not to go about in society and say witty things and have the gossip passed on to one and then to hasten next door to pass it on again; this is not living, it's clinging to the side of an iceberg.

I have no talents other than to dress; my genius is in the wearing of clothes, how am I to express it in the solitude of my chamber?

Mirror.

AUSTIN wheels a cheval glass across. BRUMMELL inspects his right profile, grunts approval. Austin angles it to show his left profile. Again BRUMMELL likes what he sees.

Good. Excellent. Very fine.

AUSTIN wheels the glass to the side.

Slippers, now. I think the –

AUSTIN: Red velvet?

AUSTIN casually tosses him a pair of red velvet slippers – the only ones that BRUMMELL has. They land on the floor. BRUMMELL looks pained.

BRUMMELL: In a few moments you will dress me to receive the Prince.

AUSTIN: King –

BRUMMELL: *(Exasperated.)* England's Kings are ten a penny – there's been only one Prince Regent –

You will dress me. There is no more intimate act that one man can perform for another – unless they both be practitioners of the Spanish Vice. There is no more important moment of the day than this. Each thing we wear says something irrevocable about us. Each choice is an autograph on a moment of time that will never be regained.

Lay out my choices.

AUSTIN: It'll be the same as yesterday.

BRUMMELL: Lay them out.

AUSTIN: And the day before.

BRUMMELL: Lay them out, sir!

AUSTIN tosses a pair of threadbare black pants on the back of the chair. BRUMMELL seems to be in a more cheerful mood at once.

I've known the Prince since Eton. I was the first man into his chamber after the wedding night – that disaster drew us even closer.

'Come back to England with me' he'll say. *'We need you.'* There is a Romantic mood afoot, there. Society has begun to worship the picturesque, the untamed, the

16

triumph of Nature over Art. The young wish to climb crags, experience Terror, *feel.* I was never much of a one for feeling; terror for me was snuff on my waistcoat or a missing button.

AUSTIN: We're going back, right. Just as long as I know. I can get packing.

Energized, he rubs his hands together, ready to start their preparations for departure –

BRUMMELL: Sentiment always leads to disorder in dress. Look at Byron. Look at Shelly. Not a crease between them. No man can allow his bosom to heave with feeling and tie his stock at the same time.

England needs me.

Yes, pack.

AUSTIN's stopped dead –

AUSTIN: Pack what?

BRUMMELL: The trunks.

AUSTIN: We don't have any and there'd be hardly anything to put in them if we had.

BRUMMELL: This could be the making of you, too.

AUSTIN: Oh yes?

BRUMMELL: A valet trained by Brummell himself? Who has been privileged to attend on me every day for the last few months –

AUSTIN: A year. Without pay.

BRUMMELL: Consider it an apprenticeship.

AUSTIN: Or slavery.

BRUMMELL: They'll seek you out, ask you my secrets. How much starch for the collar? The exact width of the pants leg?

Painful though it is to have to admit it – you will be my sartorial executor. The baton – shudder though I do to think it – falls to you.

AUSTIN: There'd be money in it?

BRUMMELL: *(Ignores it.)* My health has always been suspect. I once caught a cold from having to share an inn room with a damp stranger. Last winter nearly finished me off –

AUSTIN: It's this one I'm worried about. And again –

Another sheet of paper.

BRUMMELL: What are these?

AUSTIN: Legal documents. Don't worry about it.

BRUMMELL signs.

BRUMMELL: This Winter, sir, we shall be in England. England.

Brooks. White's. Piccadilly. The Mall. Hyde Park. Guthrie's of Cork Street. Devonshire House. The carriages. The court. All that *brilliance.*

AUSTIN: Not Italy, then? Like you said. Or Spain? Somewhere warm?

BRUMMELL: We shall be basking in the radiance of Majesty.

AUSTIN: I like the sound of that.

(Cautious.)

You're not just having one of your turns again, are you?

BRUMMELL pauses by the tall casement windows. They're too grimed to see through. He looks around for something to clean them with, finds a handful of papers.

BRUMMELL: I shall be standing there. He will look up and –

He looks more closely at the paper.

(reads.)

'*Attention, les citoyens de Calais. Le Milord Brummell invite vous a son levee –*'

AUSTIN tries to grab the papers from him but BRUMMELL pushes him away.

What is this?

AUSTIN: French.

BRUMMELL: *(Reads.)*

'Le plus famous et celebre Milord Anglais est maintenant dans Calais pour un temps limitee.

Il est dans son chambre a neuf heurs et vous est wilkommen de regardez son habitaments –'

You intended to charge admission to watch me dress?

AUSTIN: You don't get something for nothing any more, do you, since the War?

They wouldn't be allowed to touch you –

Indicates a line on the handbill –

(Reads.)

'Le touche de le Milord est verboten absolutement.'

BRUMMELL: *(Weakly.)* You're fired, get out.

AUSTIN: Fired?

AUSTIN is hurt.

Five sous per head, say twenty people a day – a handshake an extra sous.

BRUMMELL: A handshake?

AUSTIN: You wouldn't want them to kiss you, would you?

BRUMMELL: You're dismissed, didn't you hear?

AUSTIN: I had to do *something.*

BRUMMELL: To make a show of me, a display.

AUSTIN: You did the same in England.

BRUMMELL: Now and again men of distinction, of taste, of refinement – the nobility, often, occasionally royalty too, yes, would express a wish to observe me as I dressed. A very different thing from turning me into a carnival attraction.

AUSTIN: It would be done very tastefully. I was going to hire a harpsichord.

BRUMMELL: Dear God in Heaven, have not enough humiliations been heaped on my head?

AUSTIN: You don't help yourself. Those begging letters you wrote –

BRUMMELL: *(Stiffly.)* I wrote no begging letters –

AUSTIN: You mightn't call them that but people sent you money and what did you spend it on?

BRUMMELL: Essentials.

AUSTIN: Gloves, snuff, eau de cologne –

BRUMMELL: Essentials, yes.

AUSTIN: Somebody sent you a perfectly good nightshirt, what did you do? You threw it out of that window.

BRUMMELL: Cotton. It was cotton. A gentleman wears silk.

AUSTIN: You see? You see? They try to help you, you cut them dead –

BRUMMELL: Why should I be at home in Calais to someone I wouldn't receive in London?

AUSTIN: Someone asks you to take tea with them, what did you say to them? – *You take medicine, you take a walk* –

BRUMMELL: *You drink tea* –

AUSTIN: You see?

BRUMMELL: Well you do.

AUSTIN: That's not the point.

BRUMMELL: A valet does not decide what the point is. *Valet. A man-servant performing duties chiefly relating to the person of his master; a gentleman's personal attendant.*

AUSTIN: That's you all over.

BRUMMELL: What?

AUSTIN: *'You take tea'.* Trying to be clever. Trying to be funny.

BRUMMELL: Wasn't it?

AUSTIN: It was mildly amusing.

BRUMMELL: Thank you.

AUSTIN: But where did it get you?

BRUMMELL: Get me?

AUSTIN: They were good for a couple of bob. And tea.

BRUMMELL: You think I could have stopped myself saying it?

AUSTIN: Yes.

BRUMMELL: You would, of course – you've probably never said a witty thing in your life, have you?

AUSTIN: When would I get the chance? Working here?

AUSTIN gives up, indicates the dressing gown –

The black pants?

BRUMMELL: I think so, don't you?

AUSTIN: They're all you've got. When they go, that's it.

A beat –

BRUMMELL: Out of interest – interest only – exactly how many tickets have you sold?

AUSTIN: None. Le milord who? That's what they ask. *Le famous and celebre Milord Brummell,* I tell them. Blank stares. Total incomprehension.

BRUMMELL: It's your French.

AUSTIN: Hired a boy to make the pitch. They laughed at him.

BRUMMELL: No one had heard of me?

AUSTIN: Some of them had. But why throw away five good sous on a madman?

BRUMMELL: I am not mad.

AUSTIN: It's just the impression they've got –

BRUMMELL: I grant you, living like this might make one mad.

AUSTIN: You never going out, and that –

BRUMMELL: Having a valet like you would make one mad.

AUSTIN: All these imaginary visitors –

BRUMMELL: Is that what your purpose is in staying with me? To make me mad?

AUSTIN: These long conversations with the Prince of Wales –

BRUMMELL: He was my personal friend, for over twenty years.

AUSTIN: But the conversations with him? At long distance?

BRUMMELL: You're incompetent, that's the root of it – it's the root of all our problems. No fire in the grate, half the time there's no food –

AUSTIN: You go and find it.

BRUMMELL: *(Shocked.)* The son of the confidential Secretary to Lord North, Joint Receiver of the Duties on Inhabited Houses in London and Middlesex, Comptroller of the Hawkers and Peddlers Office, Agent and Paymaster to the Out-Pensioners of Chelsea Hospital and Agent to the Navy does not scavenge for food.

Get on your feet and start packing.

AUSTIN: There's nothing to pack, hardly.

BRUMMELL: Then empty the bath.

AUSTIN: You fired me.

BRUMMELL: The bath, sir!

Reluctantly, AUSTIN gets to his feet, takes the jug and starts to empty the bath. He throws the water out of the window, with a warning shout of 'Gardez l'eau!'. The action is continuous with the dialogue.

This is how the French Revolution started. With men questioning the duties and privileges of the estate they'd been born into.

AUSTIN: I know all about the duties – it's the privileges I'm short of. *Gardez l'eau!*

BRUMMELL: You're unhappy because you fill your head with these impractical schemes for making your fortune.

AUSTIN: I'm unhappy because I haven't been paid for a year. *Gardez l'eau!*

BRUMMELL: Be content with the class into which the Almighty has seen fit to place you.

AUSTIN: I'm unhappy because I'm looking after a man who argues with the Prince of Wales and other members of the English nobility all day. In his head. *Gardez l'eau!*

Bored with the argument, BRUMMELL turns back to the question of his clothes –

BRUMMELL: I approve the trousers. A good start. You're improving. What else?

AUSTIN: The problem with the French of course is they never finish anything. *Gardez l'eau!* Even the meat's always half done.

BRUMMELL: What else?

AUSTIN: Maybe they should have another Revolution. Finish the job. Maybe we should have one in England.

BRUMMELL: Is that it? Just trousers?

AUSTIN: *'The bath, sir!'*

Gardez l'eau!

The boot would be on the other foot then, wouldn't it?

He tosses a long black coat onto the chair.

It's not my fault it didn't work. You're just not a <u>draw</u>.

BRUMMELL: We shall see how much a draw I am when under Royal patronage again.

AUSTIN: We could have made a lot of money off the English lessons, too –

BRUMMELL: I don't wish to talk about those.

AUSTIN: That could have been a winner. Ten sous an hour, an hour of conversation with an English Milord –

BRUMMELL groans, starts to scrub the remaining grime from the windows. AUSTIN keeps emptying the bath, bitter.

We had them lined up on the stairs. What did you do? Ignore them. Talk over their heads to the invisible Duke of this and the imaginary Earl of that until they left here in fear of their lives.

BRUMMELL: How is one to make conversation with a Frenchman who has six words of English?

AUSTIN: Slowly.

BRUMMELL: '*Brummell!*' he'll say '*Beau!*'

AUSTIN: And if he doesn't?

BRUMMELL: Don't say that.

AUSTIN: He mightn't even recognize you.

BRUMMELL: He will.

AUSTIN: Might just ride on by. Teach you a lesson.

BRUMMELL: Of course he will.

AUSTIN gets another idea.

AUSTIN: Mud. Bath Mud. That's it. You put it around that it isn't the water that performs the cure – it's the mud.

BRUMMELL: How could he not?

AUSTIN: You put it in jars, a penny a jar, call it – Bath Mud.

BRUMMELL: Have I changed?

He rushes to the cheval glass.

AUSTIN: No, hang on, I've got it – Brummell's Medicinal Bath Mud.

BRUMMELL: I haven't changed –

AUSTIN: We'll have your face on each pot, your signature –

BRUMMELL: The best head in England, they said –

AUSTIN is scribbling feverishly in the notebook –

AUSTIN: A penny a pot, say a thousand pots a week –

BRUMMELL: *(Relieved.)* They were right.

AUSTIN: It soon adds up.

Another sheet of paper. BRUMMELL hesitates before signing

BRUMMELL: There are an extraordinary amount of these.

AUSTIN: Shouldn't have got your affairs in such a mess, should you?

He whisks the papers away

BRUMMELL: It'll be like a wretched dream, living here, among the French – dear god, the French –

(An idea.)

I should publish my memoirs.

AUSTIN: A halfpenny here, a halfpenny there –

BRUMMELL: How much do you think they'd be worth?

AUSTIN: The pots?

BRUMMELL: My memoirs.

(Beat.)

Publish? They may have beggared me but I'm still a gentleman.

AUSTIN: Everybody else does it.

BRUMMELL: But I'm Brummell.

AUSTIN: What good has it done you?

The bells ring again. Brummell screams again, furiously flings the casement open. Outside we see a small balcony with wrought iron railings.

BRUMMELL: Day and night, night and day those damn bells. Better a poorhouse than this. Better the lowest hovel in the stews of London. Better they find me lying in a ditch, better I jump off London Bridge-

AUSTIN: Get away from the window –

BRUMMELL: There is no country in the world which treats its men of genius as shamefully as England. It mocks them, spurns them, beggars them, exiles them. It can't wait to see them fall and be trampled in the mud –

AUSTIN: You're making a spectacle of yourself again.

BRUMMELL: *Too clever by half. Too big for his boots. Who does he think he is?* Let a man rise above the herd, let him bring something original into the world and they'll not rest until he's brought low, as if they can't bear the thought that someone might not be of the same dull clay as they're made of; they'll call their hatred of excellence *a distaste for show* and their malice *democracy* and if the fount of all that's gross and vulgar in them, the court, can be persuaded to join the fray, their quarry doesn't stand a chance –

AUSTIN grabs him by the waist, tries to haul him away from the window. BRUMMELL holds tight to the window jambs.

Why shouldn't he trample me into the mud? Isn't that what he's done, in all but name, all these years?

(Calls out.)

Citoyens de Calais! Observez vous le Milord Brummell! Dans un moment je intende de plonger dans la rue! Witnessez vous le moment final d'un homme Anglais meurtre par le plus grand savage, le rogue premiere de Europe, le Prince de Wales!

He steps onto the balcony, gives a scream to nerve himself to hurl himself into the street. AUSTIN thinks fast. Lets go of him, rushes to the door, announces –

AUSTIN: The Duke of Devonshire!

BRUMMELL: What?

AUSTIN: The Duke of Devonshire's come to see you.

BRUMMELL: He wasn't due to next week.

AUSTIN: Couldn't wait.

BRUMMELL hesitates, turns away, grips the railings, once more screaming to give himself the courage to jump.

The Earl of Atholl.

BRUMMELL: Who?

AUSTIN: The Marquis of Londonderry. The Great Cham of China. The Grand Mufti of Jerusalem.

Is sir at home for his lordship?

BRUMMELL: What?

AUSTIN: Dark pants with understrap, dark coat, six buttons, white shirt with muslin stock? Will that do?

A final hesitation from BRUMMELL. He unhooks his leg from the railing, heads inside again, looking confused.

Well well, look who's here.

BRUMMELL: My dear Devonshire, come in, come in.

AUSTIN: Shall I let the Duke of Norfolk out?

BRUMMELL: By all means, yes – Devonshire, you know Norfolk, I believe. He was just – ah – just –

AUSTIN: Just leaving.

BRUMMELL: He was just leaving.

BRUMMELL looks momentarily confused.

BRUMMELL: *(Cont'd.)* I was saying to Norfolk –

(to AUSTIN.) What was I talking to Norfolk about?

AUSTIN: Mud. Bath Mud. Revolution. Starch.

BRUMMELL: The other servants – where are the other servants?

AUSTIN: Day off.

BRUMMELL: All of them?

AUSTIN: They got burned to death in a big fire this morning.

AUSTIN goes to the window. He calls down.

AUSTIN *(Cont'd.)*Nothing to worry about. *Finis. (Revolves his finger at the side of his head.)*

Le Milord est un peu malade.

He slams the windows shut, gets his breath back from another near miss.

AUSTIN: *(Cont'd.)*It really can't go on like this.

BRUMMELL: Can I offer you something, Norfolk?

AUSTIN: Devonshire.

BRUMMELL: What will you have?

AUSTIN: *(Sarcastic.)* I think there's a jeroboam of champagne left and a roast swan.

BRUMMELL: No vegetables, of course. I once ate a pea. I have no intention of repeating the experiment.

AUSTIN goes to the cupboard, takes out a piece of rancid cheese and some red wine. He sets them in front of BRUMMELL, who is every inch the gracious and expansive host as Austin starts packing the few items they'll be taking with them.

There isn't much to pack – odd shoes, a broken umbrella, some tattered books and Austin's own single change of threadbare clothes. He gathers them from all over the room, stuffing them into an empty flour sack, as he responds to BRUMMELL.

Can't ask you to stay too long, Devonshire.

Drops his voice, addressing AUSTIN/DEVONSHIRE –

Expecting Royalty. I know I can rely on your discretion. I'll be back in England tomorrow.

AUSTIN: We'd better be.

BRUMMELL: You believed that the rupture between the Prince and I was final?

He has no more loyal subject than me. I would have been the first to spring to his defense should Napoleon have gained the Channel. *Fix bayonets. Hold your ground. Fire at sixty paces.* I had some ideas about a uniform, too. Isn't scarlet a little, well, *conspicuous*?

AUSTIN: He's the biggest wastrel who ever lived.

BRUMMELL: There have been some questions raised about his lifestyle, granted –

AUSTIN: Half of England's starving and he spends thousands on having a good time.

BRUMMELL: He does live with a certain *spaciousness,* true –

AUSTIN: He's fat. Immoral. Daft.

BRUMMELL: And what of it?

Princes are not put there to be models for good behavior – if that was so, what would the priests and parsons be for?

AUSTIN: He's a troublemaker.

BRUMMELL: His Lordship goes too far.

AUSTIN: He's a right bastard.

BRUMMELL: He has been, yes, it's fair to say, the fount of all corruption and disquiet in our political life for thirty years; he's an enemy to truth and decency in all its forms; he brought his own father to the grave in madness; he's the despair of his mother; he's put a wife from him in conditions which made him a laughing stock across the world but what are they to his virtues?

AUSTIN: Virtues?

BRUMMELL: Could any other man have given us the Brighton Pavilion?

AUSTIN: Or mass starvation? What about the weavers?

BRUMMELL: What are a couple of thousand starving weavers to the Music Room of that building? If we are to have a monarchy we can't have one at no expense.

AUSTIN: We pay for it all.

BRUMMELL: Money well spent.

AUSTIN: There's men with bits missing all over England. They fought for him. Now they're starving to death.

BRUMMELL: What would be the price of lifting them out of their misery at the expense of the Prince's picture collection?

AUSTIN: Whatever it was, it wouldn't be too much.

BRUMMELL: Sweep the streets clean of beggars and you sweep the walls of our Palaces clean of paintings.

AUSTIN: We can't have both?

BRUMMELL: A man suffers, his suffering is individual, private, fleeting. A collection of paintings such as the Prince chooses with his unerring eye is permanent.

AUSTIN: So's a beggar's grave.

BRUMMELL: In two hundred years a suffering man is as what? Dust. But a thing of beauty like a canvas of Reynolds or a West –

AUSTIN: And that makes it all right, does it?

BRUMMELL: There will always be one legged men in the world, there will always be poverty – how else can a man with one leg live except in poverty? – it's preposterous for him to expect anything else – but it's his children I'm thinking about –

AUSTIN: Me too.

BRUMMELL: How will their life be made better by exterminating all beauty, all Art?

AUSTIN: Why not ask them?

BRUMMELL: A Prince reminds us there is such a thing as Posterity; that we hold Art in trust for it.

A beat –

But then, you're a valet. If a terrible one.

AUSTIN: You see that?

He stops packing and indicates the bust of Homer on its stone pediment.

I'd be doing everyone a favor if I dropped that on his head as he goes by. Sixty pounds of Carrera marble'd finish him off.

BRUMMELL: The Duke of Devonshire turned Jacobin?

AUSTIN: Be quite fitting, wouldn't it? Him being such a patron of the arts and that.

BRUMMELL: *(uneasy.)* The Duke is jesting, of course.

AUSTIN: His father did for mine in the American War, Sixty Fifth Regiment of Foot, Saratoga. One of my brothers lost a leg at Badajoz and the other his life at Waterloo, fighting for that fat bastard.

Think of the amount of human bloody misery that tub of lard has caused. We'll top him here and now.

BRUMMELL: You've been abroad too long, my lord –

AUSTIN: I'm not your bloody lord.

BRUMMELL: The Republican sentiments of this wretched country are enough to turn even a ducal head –

AUSTIN: I'm not a Duke.

BRUMMELL: Moderation, that is what we must struggle for – in our dress, in politics, in everything.

AUSTIN: You don't think, if we were to drop that on his head and every single one of the upper classes was to have his throat cut, we'd all be better off?

BRUMMELL: That's what the French believed and look at them.

AUSTIN: *(Disgust.)* The French –

BRUMMELL: Limits should be set on anarchy – as on stylistic excess. In the long run neither do anyone any good.

AUSTIN: You ever looked at a rotten old cheese through a magnifying glass? You see all these maggots, filthy things, worms, crawling around. That's England.

BRUMMELL: The cure may be worse than the disease.

AUSTIN: Something has to be done. Things have to change.

BRUMMELL: Then change those things that can be changed. Take the stock. What was it but a shapeless piece of none too clean linen at one's neck until I starched it? What were pantaloons but crumpled lengths of fabric until I added straps under the heel to keep them tight?

There's work to be done yet. Take the wig.

AUSTIN: The wig?

BRUMMELL: Is there anything more calculated to turn the stomach than the habit of wearing a wig until the very lice themselves throw up their hands in horror?

Weeks, months, years go by before the thing is cleaned; you might as well wear a chamberpot on your head; how absurd you look caught in the rain, holding tight to it in case it blows away; how pitiful you look to the ladies when you exchange it for a nightcap in bed. What man can give a good account of himself in amorous combat wearing a nightcap?

Another money-making idea has flashes across AUSTIN's ever searching mind –

AUSTIN: I've got it. Rent-A-Wig. Instead of buying a wig for the season, you rent one.

AUSTIN starts to figure in his notebook again.

Buy a second hand wig for ten guineas –

BRUMMELL: Given his head the Englishman would strut in finer feathers than any man in Europe.

AUSTIN: Say one pound per week rental charge, offices in London, Brighton, Bath –

BRUMMELL: One thinks one has the Englishman brought to heel – *into your black coat, sir – into your black pants and clean white shirt* – turn your back and – horror!

Mirror. Tweezers.

AUSTIN hands the mirror and tweezers to him –

Been to Brighton?

AUSTIN: Can't say I have.

BRUMMELL: *(With all seriousness.)* It's a very pleasant day out.

Looks more closely at the mirror –

Your thumbprint is on the mirror. How often must I tell you?

BRUMMELL starts to meticulously groom every stray hair from his eyebrows and chin as AUSTIN stuffs more items into the sack – some torn underdrawers, a teacup, a battered vase.

Remember? – you must do – poor old Henry Cope, the
Green Man of Brighton? Green pants, green everything,
even dyed his hair green?

'Poodle' Byng and 'Apollo' Raikes and 'Kangaroo' Cooke
– let all the kangaroos out of the zoo to draw attention to
himself when his costume didn't –

AUSTIN: It could be a gold mine.

*Another sheet of paper. This time after BRUMMELL signs it he keeps
it in his hand, ignoring AUSTIN's attempts to take it back*

BRUMMELL: 'Romeo' Coates – meet him ever?

AUSTIN: A bloody gold mine –

BRUMMELL: As you know, his father left him a fortune in
diamonds which he had sewn all over his clothes –

AUSTIN: *(Wonderingly.)* There's money to be made everywhere,
if you put your mind to it.

BRUMMELL: They would do what they could to be noticed;
they cared not how ridiculous they made themselves if
only someone would look at them; that was their passion,
to be looked at, to be known, for anything at all, no matter
how absurd.

Brush.

AUSTIN: Everywhere except here.

BRUMMELL: Brush.

AUSTIN: *Calais.*

BRUMMELL: Brush.

AUSTIN: What a dump.

BRUMMELL: Brush.

AUSTIN: What is the *point* of Calais?

BRUMMELL: BRUSH!

AUSTIN hands it to him. BRUMMELL looks at it closely.
Filthy.

He pulls hairs out it, then rubs his skin vigorously with it.
I tamed them, sir. I made the Fops look ridiculous. I took
that English peacockery in hand.

AUSTIN: *(He's heard all this before.)* Here we go again –

BRUMMELL: The lower classes of England are always one rise in the price of bread away from uproar. The middling classes fritter their wealth on drink and display and as for the excesses of Society –

AUSTIN has taken enough, he's near to breaking point –

AUSTIN: I've got to get out. I've got to get out –

BRUMMELL: They're a race of beef eaters and brandy drinkers, the youngest child at school starts his day with a quartern of beer.

AUSTIN: I'd rather sleep on the bloody street again –

BRUMMELL: They are also known across Europe for the laxity of their sexual mores.

Personally I agree with Lord Chesterfield that the sexual act is to be avoided – the position is ridiculous, the expense exorbitant and the pleasure transitory and there's also the chance of getting your pants creased – but the Englishman and woman are at it like knives because there's something at heart *immoderate* about them.

AUSTIN: I'd rather beg.

BRUMMELL heads to the cheval glass, admiring his profiles –

BRUMMELL: A man wearing simple clothes, clean linen, nothing too tight or too fashionable, nothing which draws attention to itself or the wearer – the wearer himself, carrying himself with dignity, quiet, reserve – these things make him an enemy to excess – and excess is the antithesis of Style.

AUSTIN looks at BRUMMELL preening in front of the mirror.

AUSTIN: Was there ever a Mrs. Brummell, then?

BRUMMELL: What?

AUSTIN: I've been meaning to ask.

BRUMMELL: A Mrs. Brummell?

AUSTIN: You can see why people would wonder about that.

BRUMMELL: I can?

AUSTIN: For a man to devote every waking hour of his life to how he looks in a mirror – well, there's a hint of something unnatural there, isn't there?

BRUMMELL: Is there?

AUSTIN: Not that I'm suggesting –

(Beat.)

So there wasn't? A Mrs. B?

BRUMMELL: I was once challenged to a duel. I arrived at the appointed hour, in no inconsiderable state of agitation. I waited and waited. My opponent never showed. So it was with marriage. I stood there with my pistol loaded but no takers.

AUSTIN: It's been lonely? Would you say?

BRUMMELL: How can one be lonely with a looking glass?

AUSTIN: You never felt that, say, male companionship might have been a substitute?

BRUMMELL: No.

AUSTIN: All those people you invited to watch you dress. Men.

BRUMMELL looks at him with withering contempt –

BRUMMELL: How in God's name did you become a valet? Why in God's name did I take you on?

AUSTIN: *(Defensive.)* You were lucky to get me.

BRUMMELL: I should have sent to England for someone instead of choosing from the riff raff that infests this – this – this *underarm* of Europe. Unfrocked priests, suspect choirmasters, blackmailers, every embezzler on the run from England –

AUSTIN gives as good as he's getting –

AUSTIN: Every bankrupt, card player who doesn't want to face his debtors, people who've lost their position at court by not being able to keep their mouths shut –

BRUMMELL: *(Stung, tries to ignore it.)* Are my clothes prepared?

He stares at them thrown haphazardly on the chair –

Up to your usual standard, thrown around like so much dirty washing.

BRUMMELL picks up the clothes, reverentially, as if handling something holy.

The coat. The trousers. The shirt. The waistcoat. Honest, simple, understated. All the things I tried to get the Englishman to be.

He smooths them flat, lays them on the chair, reaches for the white shirt.

Is there anything in the world more flattering to a man than a plain white shirt? What gives him more satisfaction than to feel crisp, clean linen against his skin? What's more affecting than the simple play of black or dark blue on white? Is there a bird more ridiculous than the peacock?

Expertly folds it and picks up the stock –

Ah –

He holds it to him, closes his eyes and gives a deep, contented sigh. Then he opens them and places it also on the chair.

He picks up the waistcoat, looks at it with suspicion –

The waistcoat. There's danger in the waistcoat, there's always a certain amount of swagger in it; a *have at you, sir* and *damn your eyes*. That's not what we're after. We want line, form, restraint, not an exclamation mark. One must *tame* one's waistcoat. *Down, sir, down.*

He lays it down –

One starts to dress and immediately a calm possesses one. Order is coming to one's life – to the world. Its terrors are in abeyance for the moment, the clamor of war and revolution stilled, the passions which boil within one's own breast quieted.

He takes a deep, deep breath –

Dressed, I shall look my fellow man in the eye with the quiet confidence of one who knows there is not a line, not a thread out of place.

I shall not draw attention to myself.

I shall be today who I was yesterday, who I will be again tomorrow.

I shall look my best.

Snuff.

AUSTIN hands it to him.

The taking of snuff is the Matterhorn of social skills. They will ask you how I take mine. Watch closely. The *hours* I spent on this –

He pushes the lid up with his thumb. The box is empty. BRUMMELL gives a shrill, desperate shriek.

My Martinique?

AUSTIN: You finished it days ago.

BRUMMELL: You've been at my snuff again.

AUSTIN: Never touched it.

BRUMMELL: How many times have I told you –

AUSTIN: I don't like the stuff. It's a filthy upper-class habit.

Frantic, BRUMMELL searches on the shelves, pulls drawers open, looks under the bed.

BRUMMELL: Help me look –

AUSTIN: It's gone, all of it.

BRUMMELL: It can't be.

AUSTIN: That's where my bloody wages went, up your nose.

BRUMMELL sticks his nose into the snuff box, sniffs hard.

That's disgusting.

The distraught BRUMMELL turns it upside down, taps it.

BRUMMELL: I taught an entire generation how to take snuff –

He turns it the right way up, flips it open with his thumb again.

They copied the way I opened the box, everything. I was the Beethoven of snuff.

BRUMMELL closes his eyes. Again there's music, voices, laughter in a distant, crowded room as the lighting state changes.

The Argyle Rooms...

The Prince is expressly not invited...

Music. Art. Poetry...

'Who's your fat friend, Alvaney?'

Silence. An intake of breath. Someone drops a tray of glasses. The Prince staggers. There's a curious metallic taste in my mouth. I know that nothing will ever be the same. Someone walks face first into a pillar in astonishment. It is, I think, the sublimest moment of my life. It is also, of course, the worst.

The music dies, the light state resumes. As he hands the sheet of paper to AUSTIN he hesitates. There's something on the back of it.

BRUMMELL: What is this?

AUSTIN: Somebody's been scribbling on it. Here –

He tries to grab it but BRUMMELL snatches it back.

BRUMMELL: An engraving of – who is this –? Is that meant to be me?

AUSTIN: Nothing like you.

He tries to grab it again but again BRUMMELL snatches it back.

BRUMMELL: "*The Dandy In Exile. Number One in a Series of Satirical Sketches.*" How many of them are there?

Enraged, disbelieving, he starts to search the room.

AUSTIN: Two or three? A dozen? Couple of hundred? A few gross? One or two thousand?

BRUMMELL finds several boxes of similar sheets in various places in the room.

BRUMMELL: What in the name of –?

AUSTIN: Hogarth. *The Rake's Progress.* That's where I got the idea. You know how many they shifted of those at a shilling each? It starts off with him having a quick feel of a young lady and ends up with him in – well a madhouse – just like – only it was doxies that brought him down and in your case – *(Hastily.)* – the lunatic asylum's daughter draws and paints a bit – when you was out cold the other day she slipped in and did a few sketches. Unfortunately you woke up raving and she had to get out fast and did the rest from memory.

37

BRUMMELL: Memory of what?

AUSTIN: You.

BRUMMELL: This is not me.

AUSTIN: Not to the life, no, but it's still a warning –

BRUMMELL: A warning?

AUSTIN: Look at this – *(He scribbles in a notebook.)* – a shilling each – cost of engraving and printing, call it six pence, shipping and distribution, say, three ha'pence, the rest is yours, minus representation and management.

BRUMMELL: Representation and what?

AUSTIN: You need somebody to negotiate on your behalf, don't you? I've got to be cut in for something. It's only fair.

BRUMMELL: Who did you negotiate with?

AUSTIN: The person holding the rights to the engraving.

BRUMMELL: Who is that?

AUSTIN: Me.

BRUMMELL: You?

AUSTIN: I can't give them away for nothing. You wouldn't want that.

BRUMMELL: You will not sell my image – even as approximate as that one is – to the Mob.

(He rips the sheet he's holding to shreds.)

BRUMMELL: Give me the rest of them –

AUSTIN: Celebrity.

BRUMMELL: What?

He advances on AUSTIN who dodges out of the way, preventing him from taking the sheets.

AUSTIN: *Celebrity*. Actors. Duchesses. Royalty. Murderers. Opera-singers. Handbills, sketches of them, all over the place, selling like hotcakes, making money for somebody. Why not Brummell, too, why not The Beau?

BRUMMELL: Celebrity is for those who have done something, even if it was only to cut the throats of their wives and children –

AUSTIN: You would be *A* celebrity. Famous just for being a celebrity.

BRUMMELL: There is no such thing in the language as *A celebrity*. English doesn't work like that.

AUSTIN: You could be the first.

BRUMMELL: For what? Fame without achievement? Reputation without substance?

AUSTIN: That's not what you think of yourself, is it?

BRUMMELL: It is what the world thinks of me and to risk its scorn by the publication of this – this –

He inspects one of the sheets he's seized.

BRUMMELL: Mind you – she has caught *something* – the fold of the stock – the drape of the pant – the attitude –

AUSTIN: The attitude. That's what she got. From memory, at that. When you was asleep, at that. You were sort of giving off something that she was able to get down on paper. And at a shilling per sheet –

BRUMMELL: You think they'd sell?

AUSTIN: What are you famous for? For being famous. Now you'd be famous for being famous for being famous. You'd invent a whole new way of being in the public eye. So what if there's no such thing as *A celebrity?* Why not show the way?

He pushes the pen into BRUMMELL's hand and edge him into a chair, setting a tall pile of sheets in front of him.

AUSTIN: Make the signature nice and big. The mugs'll go for that.

After a hesitation BRUMMELL starts to sign. AUSTIN slips sheet after sheet to him, hands him new pens when needed and fills the ink well when it runs dry, anxious to keep him signing.

AUSTIN: Say something witty, now.

BRUMMELL: Just like that?

AUSTIN: Go on.

BRUMMELL: I couldn't.

AUSTIN: Just for me.

BRUMMELL: Something witty?

AUSTIN: Teach me how to say something witty.

BRUMMELL: You're a valet – why should you need to?

AUSTIN: It must be wonderful to be able to come up with something like that.

BRUMMELL: You don't 'come up' with it – it comes up with you.

AUSTIN: There's a trick to it. There must be a trick.

BRUMMELL: A trick?

AUSTIN: Go on. Do it.

BRUMMELL: Do it?

AUSTIN: Be witty.

BRUMMELL: You misunderstand the nature of the thing. Besides, my wit was more an *attitude*. There was one occasion, while staying at a country house, when I rang the fire bell by accident. The entire house was on the lawn, in night shirts, when I walked out, perfectly composed. They *applauded* me. The attitude, you see, the *effect*. That's something a valet, with all respect, couldn't pull off.

AUSTIN: I might, one day.

BRUMMELL: You would have to apprentice yourself to Wit, as you would to Style. You would try to establish a reputation in the provinces – Bristol, the Spas, then move to London.

(An aching sigh.)

London.

If you can get noticed there, you're made. All it takes is one quip which captures the public imagination and if you never say anything the rest of your life, no one will notice.

You will go to the coffee houses and keep your mouth firmly closed. You will go home and practise the witty things you hear, in your chambers. You will go to the playhouse not for the play but for what really matters, the interval; where the play is accepted for what it really is, an opportunity for you to show your own brilliance at the author's expense.

You will listen as someone's life work and a company of actor's honest efforts are shredded by a well chosen phrase. You will learn that no matter what one thinks of a piece, it is what one thinks of a piece that matters, not the piece itself.

By the end of the first speech you will have already decided what you think of the play and spend the rest of the time trying to find a phrase that will destroy it and everybody involved with it.

Then and only then will you be ready to enter Society and the Company of Wits.

AUSTIN: Attitude. Practise. Attitude.

Beat.

BRUMMELL: I fear, however, there's something too earnest about you to make it. Earnestness is Death to Style. All this talk about revolution – get that out of your head first – where did twenty-five years of upheaval get the French?

AUSTIN: They're different. They're – French.

You still believe in Monarchy? After what you've been through?

BRUMMELL: Ever been to a concert? Mozart, Hayden? Half the orchestra will be drunks or wife beaters, the concert master will have a thing for little boys. Do we care? It's the music we like. It's the same with the English and monarchy. It's the *idea* of it that matters, not whatever squalid wretch happens to be sitting on the throne.

My connection with the Prince could, of course, have made me rich. I had access, influence, *grease.*

Bowing low, as if the Prince is in front of him –

'Might I suggest, Your Highness, that sixteen rows of medals are a little too much – and I have a friend who is interested in the post of Hereditary Beekeeper –'

Straightening up –

I left the Court poorer than when I was taken up by it. Did I ask for a peerage? A pension? A sinecure? Did I profit by it in any way at all?

AUSTIN: You're doing it to yourself again –

BRUMMELL: *(agitated.)*

Look at Fortnum. Look at Mason. They're doing all right for themselves, aren't they? I gave the court Style and Wit, the twin of Style –

AUSTIN: Have some cheese – and if these prints sell –

BRUMMELL: What's my reward? This. Here. You. Exile. *Calais*. Rumors that my mind has been affected, my senses overthrown –

He grabs the cheese knife which AUSTIN is about to use, holds it at his throat –

It's not to be borne –

AUSTIN: Put it down –

BRUMMELL: I've lost everything –

AUSTIN: Put the cheese knife down –

BRUMMELL looks at the knife. There's a little bit of cheese sticking to it. He pops the cheese into his mouth, swallows, holds the knife to his throat again.

BRUMMELL: My snuff – my Martinique –

He screams, trying to get the courage to slash –

AUSTIN: Don't –

BRUMMEL screams, once more tries to nerve himself to slash –

(Bitter.)

Kill yourself and I'll have to carry the can –

BRUMMELL: It's about you all the time, isn't it?

He screams again, still can't bring himself to slash. AUSTIN bows to the door –

AUSTIN: The Duke of Devonshire –

BRUMMELL: Where?

AUSTIN: At the door.

BRUMMELL: He left.

AUSTIN: Norfolk, then –

BRUMMELL: You *are* Norfolk –

AUSTIN: Am I?

AUSTIN can't face anymore, paces around the room as if he'd like to beat his brains out on the walls –

(Explosive, desperate.)

I've got to go. I've got to go. I've got to get out of here. I've got to get away.

There's the sound the booming of a cannon in the distance.

I can't stay here. How can I stay here? I've had it. That's it. Stay here? Here? I've got to be gone. Go. I've got to go. No, I'm going. That's it.

Another boom –

BRUMMELL: What's that?

AUSTIN: Cannon.

BRUMMELL: Cannon?

AUSTIN: Cannon. They're at it again. Another revolution. They keep trying, you have to give them that.

He takes the knife from BRUMMELL, who's intently listening –

BRUMMELL: Listen –

The distant booms continue –

(Counting.)

Three –

AUSTIN: It can't make things any worse for us, that's one consolation –

BRUMMELL: Four –

AUSTIN: When you've hit rock bottom –

BRUMMELL: Five –

AUSTIN scurries around throwing the last few items into the sack – a chipped plate, a rusted knife, a pack of tattered cards.

AUSTIN: I couldn't face last winter again –

BRUMMELL: Six –

AUSTIN: Another winter in Calais? –

BRUMMELL: Seven –

AUSTIN: England, Bath –

BRUMMELL: Eight –

AUSTIN: Just saying the words does something for you, doesn't it?

BRUMMELL: Nine –

AUSTIN: I mean say what you like –

BRUMMELL: Ten –

AUSTIN: There's nothing like it, is there?

BRUMMELL: Eleven –

AUSTIN: London –

BRUMMELL: Twelve –

AUSTIN: Can you imagine being in London again? –

BRUMMELL: Thirteen –

AUSTIN: The crowds –

BRUMMELL: Fourteen –

AUSTIN: The coffee houses –

BRUMMELL: Fifteen –

AUSTIN: The theatre –

BRUMMELL: Sixteen –

AUSTIN: There's just something about it –

BRUMMELL: Seventeen –

AUSTIN: It's a filthy hole –

BRUMMELL: Eighteen –

AUSTIN: They'd cut your throat there as soon as look at you-

BRUMMELL: Nineteen –

AUSTIN: But they're *us*, aren't they?

BRUMMELL: Twenty –

AUSTIN: We belong there –

BRUMMELL: Twenty one –

AUSTIN: Bloody *Calais*?

The booms stop –

BRUMMELL: Twenty-one. He's here. He's landed. That was
the salute.

The Prince –

In the distance we hear the sound of cheering as AUSTIN ties the sack.
(Whisper.)

The Prince –

AUSTIN: He's here. He's really here. And there's a chance he'll be dropping in, will there?

BRUMMELL: How could he not?

AUSTIN: Right then –

He drops the sack, pulls the rug up, takes out a small box hidden underneath, opens it.

AUSTIN: Let's give the bugger the welcome he deserves –

He takes out a dwelling pistol and brandishes it at the door as we –

END ACT ONE

Act Two

AUSTIN loads the pistol with powder and ball.

AUSTIN: Typical. Cheering him. Just like the bloody French. You think the English are frivolous?

The Frenchman takes a glass of red wine and says 'Let's have a Republic' and then he'll take a glass of white and say 'No, we'll have an Emperor'. They cut the head off one King, then along comes a Napoleon –

They're full of theories, you see – well, if you keep ending up in a bigger mess than when you started, you need something to explain it. Your Englishman wouldn't know a theory if it was to be served up in caper sauce but every so often he puts down his beer and astonishes the world.

He'll do it again, you'll see.

BRUMMELL: What are you doing with that?

AUSTIN: I'm not all mouth and trousers, pal. Hot Air Harry? Rabbit rabbit rabbit? When I say I'll do a thing, consider it done, matey. The guillotine? Scared of it? Me? I laugh at it, I do, I scoff.

BRUMMELL: Put that down.

AUSTIN: *(Declaims.)* Princes, the dregs of their dull race, who flow
Through public scorn, mud from a muddy spring
And leech like to their fainting country cling
Till they drop, blind in blood, without a blow.

BRUMMELL: My clothes, sir!

AUSTIN: Dress your bloody self.

BRUMMELL: My glass –

AUSTIN: You fetch it.

BRUMMELL: My brush –

Feels his chin, reassuring himself that it's smooth –

My teeth –

Blows into his cupped hand, sniffs –

Good. Fine.

My boots, are they blacked?

AUSTIN: Do I care?

BRUMMELL: He's here. The Prince is here.

His hands are shaking with nervous anticipation –

My cologne –

Picks up a cologne bottle and tries to spray himself with it. It's empty.

The apartment – tidy it.

He rushes around the room, trying to get it into some kind of order.

AUSTIN: As soon as he walks through that door –

(He aims the pistol at the door.)

Bang. Right in the chops. Straight through the gizzard.

(Gripped by sudden despair.)

Oh what's the use. This is a madhouse. You think they're going to let him come into a madhouse?

BRUMMELL: Help me.

AUSTIN: The most you can say is it's better than prison.

BRUMMELL: I was not in prison.

AUSTIN: You were in a debtor's prison for running up bills bigger than the bills you ran away from in London.

BRUMMELL: I temporarily withdrew to the country.

AUSTIN: In irons.

BRUMMELL: I was staying with friends.

AUSTIN: You don't have any.

BRUMMELL: In the country.

AUSTIN: You were in debtor's prison and it sent you mad. That's why we're here. The Sisters of Charity took you in.

BRUMMELL: It's a convent.

AUSTIN: It's a madhouse. It's almost like being in lodgings, I give you that. Except it's cheaper. And you can't get out. And everybody's mad. And I'm stuck here with you.

Indicates the door –

Open the door.

BRUMMELL: The door?

AUSTIN: If it's not a madhouse, open the door.

BRUMMELL: The draft –

AUSTIN: Go on, open it.

BRUMMELL: My papers – they'd blow everywhere –

AUSTIN: Shall I do it?

BRUMMELL: *(Panicked.)* No.

AUSTIN: I'll open the door, shall I?

BRUMMELL: I said I would dress.

AUSTIN: You'll have to face it sometime.

BRUMMELL: I had a stroke, I do remember that. It left a certain lameness in my favorite leg. I always preferred the left, somehow, don't ask me why.

AUSTIN: Nobody could blame you for going mad.

BRUMMELL: I did not go mad.

AUSTIN: Half naked, in a cell, chained up.

BRUMMELL: I was not chained up.

AUSTIN: I feel I'm going mad myself some times. Bloody Calais.

BRUMMELL: Don't you want to see England again? Bath? London?

AUSTIN: With you? Fat chance. You're mad.

BRUMMELL: I am not mad.

AUSTIN: I kept one of your letters. Thought I might be able to sell it to a newspaper. *Toff's Valet In Royal Reject's Madhouse Shocker.* No one was interested.

Pulls out a crumpled sheet of paper –

(Reads.)

'Yesterday's dinner was half the skeleton of a pigeon, more probably a crow, in rancid butter with a handful of cherries and a biscuit the size of a bad halfpenny' –

BRUMMELL: I never wrote that –

He tries to snatch it but AUSTIN pulls it away, keeps reading –

AUSTIN: *(Reads.)* *'I have been reduced, for the last eight and forty hours, to rub myself down with my dirty shirts, for want of a towel –'*

(Looks up.)

Does that sound like you?

(Reads.)

'It is impossible to find neccessaries in this hell on earth. I fear I shall have to give up the ghost from famine and filthiness.'

I do think that sounds like Beau Brummell.

BRUMMELL snatches the letter, scans it, mouth working.

The nuns took you in. That's why nobody visits. All the English here are C of E, they won't have anything to do with you.

BRUMMELL: Dirty shirts?

AUSTIN: I'm an atheist, me. Jesus Christ? I say crucify the bugger. But you can see their point.

BRUMMELL: No towel?

AUSTIN: It's a matter of national temperament.

BRUMMELL: No –

AUSTIN: You take the Frenchman – excitable, vicious, helpless in the face of feeling, addicted to sensation –

BRUMMELL gives an agonized cry and crunches the paper up.

BRUMMELL: No –

AUSTIN: He likes all that incense and ecstasy.

BRUMMELL doubles over with another cry of despair –

BRUMMELL: Nooooo –

Gets to his feet, heads to the chair with the clothes on it, as if energized by the distress he's thrown BRUMMELL into –

AUSTIN: Right, dressing gown.

BRUMMELL: *(Faintly.)* What?

AUSTIN: The dressing gown.

BRUMMELL: What?

AUSTIN: The dressing gown.

BRUMMELL: What?

AUSTIN: The dressing gown.

BRUMMELL: What?

AUSTIN: The dressing gown.

BRUMMELL: What?

AUSTIN: Are you getting bloody dressed or aren't you?

A crushed BRUMMELL stands there helplessly as AUSTIN takes the dressing gown off him.

You never know, they might let him in. Everybody likes to laugh at a lunatic. Unless he's forgotten you. You could always pray.

BRUMMELL: What?

AUSTIN: Get down on your knees, pray he remembers you.

BRUMMELL: Pray?

AUSTIN: I suppose not, no, clothes were your religion, weren't they?

BRUMMELL: *(Still faintly.)* To be dressed well, to say the right thing at the right time, that's the nearest we ever get to the divine.

AUSTIN: What about eternal life?

BRUMMELL: What, precisely, about it?

AUSTIN: If it is going to be the guillotine –

(He fingers his neck, swallows.)

Is there life after death? Why are we here? What does it mean? What is our purpose? Who are we? Is there a grand design? Is there a God? Does he care for us? You think I've never thought about things like that but I have. I've thought about them a lot. On and off.

BRUMMELL's voice still sounds weak and faint –

BRUMMELL: They have always seemed to me to be trivial speculations.

AUSTIN: Trivial?

BRUMMELL: When faced with the mysteries of dress.

AUSTIN: If there is a Hell wouldn't you be frightened to go there?

BRUMMELL: I should attempt to carry it off with style.

AUSTIN: What if there's no clean linen there? No looking glasses?

BRUMMELL: I should cope with the inconvenience.

AUSTIN: Of infinite suffering in infinite time?

BRUMMELL: Why should a valet concern himself with the infinite?

AUSTIN looks genuinely troubled –

AUSTIN: What if there is a Hell? Eh? What if we spend forever, there? What does forever mean? It means that if there was a cube of the hardest crystal a million miles on a side and every million years someone touched it, it would eventually be worn away but in that time your suffering would hardly have begun, though it had already seemed to last forever.

BRUMMELL: What a vulgar concept.

AUSTIN: It doesn't make you think?

BRUMMELL: My cap.

AUSTIN: What?

BRUMMELL: My cap and slippers.

AUSTIN: What? Oh –

AUSTIN takes the cap off his head. BRUMMELL lifts his feet for the slippers to be removed.

BRUMMELL: I really wouldn't spend any more time worrying about eternity if I was you. The English don't. We can safely leave that to the Italians.

Glass.

AUSTIN trundles a cheval glass towards him.

AUSTIN: There really is nothing going on in that head of yours when you look in a mirror, is there? Except how you look.

BRUMMELL: What harm was ever done by a man in his chambers, tying his stock? What time could be more innocently spent?

Another burst of cheering breaks out, coming nearer –

The pants –

AUSTIN: *(Needling.)* In the end, I suppose, he'll lose the urge
to leave his chamber altogether? He'll stay inside it,
holding conversations with imaginary Dukes and Earls?
Conversing, across the English channel, with the Prince of
Wales and other layabouts?

BRUMMELL: Pants?

*AUSTIN picks them up, hands them to him. BRUMMELL leans on
him as he carefully puts them on, over his drawers. AUSTIN hardly
dares hope they're actually going to get out of here –*

AUSTIN: You really think he'll want to see you again?

BRUMMELL: Why shouldn't he?

AUSTIN: Let you go back to court?

BRUMMELL: Could it possibly have been the same without me?

AUSTIN: You have a very high opinion of yourself.

BRUMMELL: There was some antique genius who put the
Roman into the toga – some Caledonian prankster the
Scotsman into his kilt – I, Brummell, put the modern
man into pants, dark coat, white shirt and clean linen; I
daresay that will be sufficient to secure my fame. Religion?
Philosophy? It would seem to me to be in the worst of
taste to trouble others with my private reflections on
them. If we're here for a purpose it's to pass through life
as elegantly as possible; to apply the imagination to life's
realities as well as its fancies; to keep ones linen clean; to
behave like a gentleman, which means never being rude
unless you mean to be and to, yes, look one's best.

AUSTIN: There is no higher purpose than that? Looking your
best?

BRUMMELL: Shirt –

Napoleon thought there was some higher purpose – and
Nero – and Caligula – and Tamberlane – and Atilla the
Hun –

*Cheering sounds from the street; still distant but getting closer.
BRUMMELL goes on the counter attack, as if he's drawing strength
from it.*

The Prince now – at least you can say about him that he's no danger to anyone. Too fat, too lazy. Can you see him on a horse? Leading a charge? Think how dangerous he would be if he woke up one morning with a *purpose*.

Shirt.

AUSTIN takes the shirt and helps him into it. BRUMMELL gives a heart felt sigh –

Oh that first chill kiss of linen on one's flesh in the morning –

AUSTIN: Hang on –

He hunts down a flea in the seams of the shirt –

I saw him jump – he's in the seam – got him –

Triumphantly he shows BRUMMELL the flea crushed between his thumb and index finger. BRUMMELL shudders.

BRUMMELL: Glass.

AUSTIN hands him the looking glass and BRUMMELL checks how he looks from the back.

What do you think?

AUSTIN: About what?

BRUMMELL: The line of the pants? The length of the cuffs?

AUSTIN: Does it matter?

BRUMMELL: At one time I considered using a different tailor for each pant's leg. Seymour's of Savile Row seemed to understand my right leg better.

AUSTIN: It looks all right from here.

BRUMMELL: *'It looks all right from here?'*

AUSTIN: What do you want me to say?

BRUMMELL: Forgive me, but I should have thought someone taking up the career of valet might have had some passing interest in clothes.

AUSTIN: It's a living. Barely.

BRUMMELL: What would you rather be doing?

AUSTIN: *O tantum libeat mecum tibi sordida rura atque humilis habitare casas et figure ceruos*

53

haedorumque gregem uiridi compellere hibisco –

BRUMMELL: *(Translating.)*

   O come and live with me in the countryside
   Among the humble farms. Together we
   Will hunt the deer and tend the little goats.

   That's a very beautiful thought.

AUSTIN: Thank you.

BRUMMELL: It really is. *The little goats.* A picture.

AUSTIN: Well that's Virgil for you, isn't it?

BRUMMELL: The best of them, I think.

AUSTIN: Juvenal, Ovid – fuck them. Virgil's the boy.

BRUMMELL: You can just see it, can't you? The way he puts it. There's something essentially English about him.

AUSTIN: He was Italian.

BRUMMELL: You know what I mean.

AUSTIN: One keeps going back to him.

BRUMMELL: One does.

AUSTIN: There's always a line, a telling phrase, a thought.

BRUMMELL: I've never been one for pastoral, myself; the countryside, what I've seen of it through a coach window, seems to be nothing but death and excrement but he almost convinces one –

AUSTIN: A country lane, a little cottage, a few goats –

BRUMMELL: *Little* goats. *Little* makes so much the difference.

AUSTIN: I knew you'd like him.

   Beat –

BRUMMELL: Of course to appreciate the man, you have to have some Latin.

AUSTIN: Latin?

BRUMMELL: You just spoke in Latin.

   AUSTIN looks panicked.

AUSTIN: Did I? Was it?

BRUMMELL: *Mecum una in siluis imittabere Pana cenedo –*

AUSTIN: *(Automatically.)*

    Pan primum calamos cera coniungere pluris–

BRUMMELL: What is a valet doing speaking Latin?

AUSTIN: I don't.

BRUMMELL: You just did.

AUSTIN: Latin? That's Latin?

AUSTIN looks wildly around, tries to explain it away.

I woke up speaking it, this morning, just like that. I picked it up a couple of days ago. My previous master was Latin. We always spoke Latin at home. Anyway, I never said anything in Latin. You must have misheard me.

Opens his mouth, closes it.

No Latin, see? Not a word.

The pants? You're maybe a half inch higher in the left leg. Sleeve length's good. The collar looks a little tight –

BRUMMELL: You never did show me your references –

AUSTIN: *(Improvising desperately.)* The ship sank that was carrying them. The post's been held up. There was a big fire the night before I was going to show them to you.

He fusses over the clothes BRUMMELL's wearing –

I couldn't get the claret stain out of the shirt. Do you want me to wash it again? The sleeves are fraying. I'll cut them off. The pants are a little shiny on the backside – try not to sit down in them-

BRUMMELL: You turned up on the doorstep. You begged me to give you the job.

AUSTIN: The bath –

He starts furiously emptying the bathwater with the jug, again with the shouts of 'Gardez l'eau!'.

BRUMMELL: Before I knew it you were shaving me. Not very well. Almost as if you'd never shaved someone before.

AUSTIN: Nerves. I'm always like that with a new master.

BRUMMELL: Who did you work for before?

AUSTIN: I forgot. I never knew. He didn't tell me. He didn't have a name. He died before he was born. I don't like to gossip.

BRUMMELL: *(Growing suspicion.)* All I know about you is that you have ideas above your station and the most violent Republican sentiments.

AUSTIN: The Latin? Don't let that fool you. I memorized it all.

(Recites.)

Pan curat ouis ouiuumque magistros
nec te paeniteat calamo truisse labellum –

I've got a very good memory, me. When I was valet to... Lord Essex, I remember him saying, what a memory you have, Austin, for a valet. Even though you don't speak Latin. Or understand it. Latin? What's that?

BRUMMELL is getting increasingly disturbed, backs away from him.

BRUMMELL: Who are you?

AUSTIN: I'll go and see about that firewood, then.

BRUMMELL grabs the breadknife, waves it at him –

BRUMMELL: Stay where you are.

AUSTIN: We're out of cheese.

BRUMMELL: Why are you here?

AUSTIN: Snuff. I'll cut my leg off and sell it for snuff.

He goes to the door, hesitates, turns –

Where would a man like me learn Latin or Greek? Where would he learn anything? In jail.

BRUMMELL: Jail?

AUSTIN: There was a riot going on about bread –

BRUMMELL: What is it with the lower classes and *bread*?

AUSTIN: I didn't know anything about it, I was minding my own business –

BRUMMELL: Which was?

AUSTIN: I don't like to say.

BRUMMELL: I think I need to know –

AUSTIN: *(Reluctant.)* It was in the leather industry –

BRUMMELL: What part of it, exactly?

AUSTIN: I was a bateman.

BRUMMELL: Which means?

AUSTIN: It's part of the business of tanning hides.

BRUMMELL: What part?

AUSTIN sighs –

AUSTIN: You have to stand in a barrel of dog shit and tread it into a mush.

BRUMMELL: All day long?

AUSTIN: It's all the work I could get. I was on my lunch break and I turned the corner and walked into this crowd, running and shouting. Next thing I know someone on a horse is swinging a sabre at me and I'm thrown in jail.

BRUMMELL: Still wearing the same shoes?

AUSTIN: I did five years. There was nothing in the cell but an old Greek and Latin primer. I read it cover to cover to keep myself sane. When they let me out I couldn't stay in England, could I? They'd marked my cards for me.

BRUMMELL: You didn't think of going back to your old trade?

AUSTIN: Would you?–

In the distance the crowd cheers again. The sound agitates and distracts BRUMMELL, who puts the knife down.

BRUMMELL: I shall be at the window when he comes. Turn slowly to greet him. *'Ah, Wales, I'll say.'* Left profile, I think.

Beat –

Or perhaps my back to him. The suggestion that I haven't quite forgiven him, not yet –

Beat –

Sitting?

He darts to the armchair, sits.

'Ah, Wales, there you are.' As if none of it had happened, or if it had, it was too insignificant to bother one.

AUSTIN: I'd heard about you, of course –

Preoccupied, BRUMMELL gets off the chair, drapes himself against the mantelpiece –

BRUMMELL: Something in between, perhaps.

AUSTIN: Who hasn't?

BRUMMELL reaches for the snuff box –

BRUMMELL: Indifference without insolence. As if he'd caught me at my snuff. *'Ah, Wales – Martinique?'*

AUSTIN: Everybody's *heard* about you –

BRUMMELL: A book?

AUSTIN: And here you were, in Calais, too –

BRUMMELL pulls a book off the shelf, opens it, places his hand on his forehead –

BRUMMELL: *(Recites.) Princes, the dregs of their dull race –*
Hastily snaps the book shut –

My boots, where are my boots?

AUSTIN: *'Who's your fat friend?'.* You were one of us, I thought –

BRUMMELL: Boots?

AUSTIN: Why would you have said it if you weren't? Ridiculed him to his face, like that?

BRUMMELL: Boots?

AUSTIN: Of course you're not, I know that now, you are just the damn fool who invented the understrap and twenty seven ways to tie a neckerchief, without a thought in his head that isn't to do with what he looks like in front of a cheval glass – but you can still turn the world upside down by helping me skewer this sod.

Hopeful again, he brandishes the pistol.

BRUMMELL: Boots?

AUSTIN: It's a chance to redeem yourself. Like all the bloody upper classes you gambled everything you had and kept on gambling and borrowing and trying to win it back and when you did you gambled it all away again, left London in the dead of night, with one pound, five shillings to

your name, beggared yourself, left your closest friends to
be ruined, bankrupted half the people you owed money
to, the things you left behind were sold by the bailiff and
if you ever went back to England you'd be thrown into
the Clink and never come out again and in the Clink, I
guarantee, you'd look back with longing at half a pigeon in
rancid butter –

BRUMMELL: Boots? Boots boots boots?

AUSTIN: I'm a fool to myself, of course, thinking you could be
anything different – the bathwater! – the fire! – snuff! –

BRUMMELL: Boooooots?

AUSTIN: You weren't with us at all, were you? How could you be?
You liked things just like they were, you didn't want a Smash.

Exasperated, BRUMMELL starts rummaging for his boots himself.

BRUMMELL: You are without doubt the worst manservant I
have ever had. Give me that weapon –

*He seizes the pistol and there's a tug of war between them during
the next speeches.*

AUSTIN: I do want a smash. One great big, marvellous,
absolutely wonderful Smash, an English revolution that'll
make up for all the time I spend inside with the same pair
of boots as the day they picked me up.

BRUMMELL: You want an English Revolution?

AUSTIN: I want somebody to pay.

BRUMMELL: We've had it.

I led it.

AUSTIN: You're just a bloody walking clothes horse.

BRUMMELL: I was the greatest Revolutionary of them all.

Before me the sign of good breeding was an extravagance
in dress – a macaronical riot of color and fabric – silks,
velvets, golden thread – a three foot high wig – I put a
stop to it. Lined up my cannon, loaded it with shot, blew
all that to smithereens. I disposed my forces. A skirmish
here. A frontal attack there. Sometimes a temporary
retreat. Then an attack from the rear. For over twenty years

I fought to drag the Englishman out of his addiction to excess. I succeeded. England lay at my feet but who did I harm to achieve my conquest? Who did I widow? What orphan curses my name? Why? Because I chose only to fight those battles which would improve the lot of man on a practical basis; political theory or ambition or national aggrandizement or the inhuman conceits of a social or economic ideal were alien to me.

The true, permanent revolutions are those of private life.

AUSTIN: You can't have a *private* revolution. The whole point of one is to knock everybody out of their armchairs – heads blown off, bits of arms and legs lying here there and everywhere – like that bastard on the horse who grabbed me that day.

BRUMMELL: You're wrong –

AUSTIN: What would you know about it?

They're both exhausted from the struggle but neither will let go of the pistol as they face each other, panting.

AUSTIN: A Bust Up, that's what we want. One huge, stupefying Bust Up –

BRUMMELL: And then what?

AUSTIN: Something like the French Revolution – only not French –

BRUMMELL: And after all the blood letting, what? You'll still be a valet and I'll still be looking for my boots –

AUSTIN: I saw the London Carlisle mail coach turn over once –

BRUMMELL: *(Reflexive.)* Carlisle – <u>uh</u>.

AUSTIN: The axle broke, up it goes in the air; luggage, people flying everywhere – down it comes, broken necks, dead horses, a ten foot hole in the road – inspiring, it was, all them smug buggers sitting there one minute, the next – hallo?

BRUMMEL finds his boots, stares at them in horror –

BRUMMELL: The soles of my boots haven't been blacked –

AUSTIN: We're out of blacking.

BRUMMELL: I can't face the Prince in unblacked boots.

AUSTIN: It's only the soles.

BRUMMELL: *(Outraged.) Only the soles?*

AUSTIN: He won't see them.

BRUMMELL: I'll know.

AUSTIN: So what?

BRUMMELL: *So what?*

AUSTIN: Your linen's filthy. Your backside is sticking out of your pants. Your shirt's got holes in it. Who cares about the soles of your boots?

BRUMMELL: *Who cares?*

AUSTIN: Nobody blacks the soles of their boots.

BRUMMELL: I do.

AUSTIN: What's the point?

BRUMMELL: The grate. Soot. Quickly.

AUSTIN: Tell me what the point is, first.

BRUMMELL: Isn't it obvious?

AUSTIN: The French Revolution. The American Revolution. The Napoleonic Wars. Moscow burned to the ground. Europe in flames from one end to the other. You lived through it all. Did you really – no, don't tell me – you really did, didn't you? – you spent all of that time looking at the soles of your boots in a mirror.

Cheering sounds from the street, getting closer. BRUMMELL rushes to the grate and uses the soot to black the bottom of his boots.

BRUMMELL: It can't go on like this.

AUSTIN: That's what I keep saying.

A final effort and BRUMMELL wrestles the pistol away from him.

BRUMMELL: I'm sorry but you'll have to go.

AUSTIN: Go where?

BRUMMELL: Take your notice.

AUSTIN: You can't do that.

BRUMMELL: *Master. One who gives directions, orders. He who is in charge.*

AUSTIN: Give it back. I'm going to put three ounces of lead through the third button of his waistcoat.

BRUMMELL: You want a Revolution?

AUSTIN: The bloodier the better.

BRUMMELL: You're going back to start one here?

AUSTIN: Best chance I got.

BRUMMELL: I couldn't be responsible for such a thing.

AUSTIN: I'd keep you out of it.

BRUMMELL: It's my lodging. You work for me.

AUSTIN takes out another sheet of paper with an illustration on it.

AUSTIN: Take a look at that. I had her knock up another one. About me, this time. About what I'm about to do. *Vice Dethroned. Or Tyranny O'erthrown by Brotherhood.*

BRUMMELL: It's very close to a likeness of you.

AUSTIN: I thought that.

BRUMMELL: And of him. You're going to cut his head off?

AUSTIN: Not with a pistol. It's allegorical.

BRUMMELL: Who's this here? Looking down? Is it meant to be me again?

AUSTIN: That's John Bellingham. The hero who shot that bloodsucker Spencer Percival down in the House of Commons.

BRUMMELL: Who?

AUSTIN: The Prime Minister.

BRUMMELL: Of –?

AUSTIN: Ours. *Our* Prime Minister. The one just after the Duke of Portland.

BRUMMELL: Percival who –?

AUSTIN: *Spencer Percival.* Bellingham popped his clogs for him. The only British Prime Minister to be assassinated. So far.

BRUMMELL: When was this?

AUSTIN: A couple of years back.

BRUMMELL: You're sure?

AUSTIN: He won't be the last.

BRUMMELL: It made the newspapers?

AUSTIN: Made the newspapers? A Prime Minister struck down in the seat of Parliament itself? The head wolf of that pack of man-eating wolves and hyenas that run this country? For a day or so, yes.

BRUMMELL: Now I think I do remember something about this but Spencer Percival was possibly the most inoffensive and mild mannered man ever to serve in government.

AUSTIN: I'm speaking allegorically.

BRUMMELL: That's right, he was shot by a lunatic who thought he'd been cheated over a government contract.

AUSTIN: A man whose name will ring through the ages, who did what he did on behalf of suffering humanity, striking the first blow for freedom of which mine will be the second. If that pistol works.

BRUMMELL: Jim Thorpington?

AUSTIN: *John* Thorpington. Frogmorton. Froginhgham. Something like that. The point is the Bust Up.

BRUMMELL: Was there one?

AUSTIN:

No but when a crowned head rolls in the dust, spurting blood –

BRUMMELL: So you are going to cut his head off? *(hastily.)* Allegorically, yes, of course – but do you know what it's like to live through a Bust Up? You should ask the *concierge* at the apartment where I first stayed in Calais. When the

Revolution broke out one of her brothers was crushed to death by the crowd rushing to storm the Bastille. Another was mistaken in the Terror for someone of the same name, denounced and guillotined before it could be cleared up. Her other brothers were forced into the army. Two of them died at Austerlitz and two froze to death on the way back from Moscow. One sister was raped by twenty cossacks when the Russians took Paris and the other by fifteen British troops after Waterloo. None of this need have happened if everybody, from Napoleon down, had spent more time in front of the mirror, or rubbed themselves for two hours each morning with a pig's-bristle brush.

AUSTIN: It wouldn't have to be the guillotine, would it?

BRUMMELL: *(Carefully tying his stock.)* Could any member of her family have dodged what was coming to them? No. But each believed their life mattered, in some way, to God or some higher purpose, there was plan in it, and meaning. They knew they weren't just caught in events but that events were caught up in *them*, that the Universe, no less than they themselves was concerned with their pathetic little destinies –

This is what the Revolution came to, cried her brother, dying in the snow on the retreat from Moscow. *This is what it was all about*, cried her sister, as the sixth or seventh Cossack thrust himself into her. As that dragoon ran you down, as the years dragged on with you chained to the wall in prison, you, too, told yourself it all had *significance,* didn't you?

AUSTIN: I'm British so they mightn't.

BRUMMELL: So they'd hang you instead.

AUSTIN: I bet they wouldn't. I bet they'd let me go. Make a hero of me. It might start a war, shooting him here. Wouldn't that be something? A wonderful, wonderful war.

BRUMMELL sets the pistol down but keeps it near to hand as we hear more cheering. It's mixed in with the sound of hooves and carriage wheels, jingling harnesses and a jaunty military march.

BRUMMELL: We have just survived, by the skin of our teeth, a fanatical age – riot, war, revolution, political theory, *enthusiasm.* It's all so much more simpler when man concentrates on the simple *getting* of things. Democracy? What is it but a communal ejaculation?

(Panting.)

'*Yes, yes, oh yes* –. What is it to do with the government what my political opinions are? Let it look after its business while I go about mine. *Virtus Sola Nobilita.*

AUSTIN: Virtue is the only nobility? I'm out to smash all nobility.

BRUMMELL: The stock? How is it?

AUSTIN: It looks all right.

BRUMMELL: *All right?*

AUSTIN: Not bad.

BRUMMELL: It's perfection. Take a look.

AUSTIN: I'm looking.

BRUMMELL: See how it falls, fold on fold, ripple on ripple from chin to shirtfront, how high it is on the neck, how close under the ears –

AUSTIN: It's a good one –

BRUMMELL: If this was a violin sonata it would be by Bach.

AUSTIN: Bach, yes – they're nearly here. The pistol –

BRUMMELL: Once in a lifetime one ties a stock this perfect –

Brushes the reflection with his fingertips –

It's almost too good to waste on him.

Reluctantly he moves away, holds his arms out –

Waistcoat!

My first tailor, Schweitzer, was asked by a customer what cloth he recommended. '*Why, sir, the Prince wears superfine and Mr. Brummell the Bath coating. Suppose, sir, we say the Bath coating? – Mr. Brummell has a trifle the preference.*'

AUSTIN: Hold still.

He helps him into the waistcoat.

BRUMMELL: *(Chuckles.)* '*A trifle the preference.*'

AUSTIN: Right –

He pushes the cheval glass back in front of BRUMMELL –

BRUMMELL: *(Anxiously.)* Yes?

AUSTIN: *Manifique.*

BRUMMELL: You don't think one shoulder is higher than the other?

AUSTIN: No.

BRUMMELL: The lapel. It's quite flat?

AUSTIN: Yes.

BRUMMELL: The coat isn't a half inch too long?

AUSTIN: No.

BRUMMELL: Or too short?

AUSTIN: No.

BRUMMELL: Is that a stain?

AUSTIN: No.

BRUMMELL: Snuff?

AUSTIN: No.

He pushes the cheval glass away.

The balcony.

BRUMMELL: What?

AUSTIN: I could pop him from there. Even if they don't let him in.

BRUMMELL: The balcony?

AUSTIN: Listen –

He goes to the window that opens onto the balcony and throws it open.

BRUMMELL: Those damn bells.

AUSTIN: I can see his coach. I think it's his coach –

The agitated BRUMMELL heads to the cheval glass again –

BRUMMELL: I can't receive him like this –

AUSTIN: Typical. We beat the bastards and now they're all over us –

BRUMMELL: Come away from that window, sir!

AUSTIN: *(Shouts, bitterly.)* Whatever happened to the Rights of Man? *Liberte, Equalite, Fraternite?* You ought to be ashamed of yourselves, *merde* to the lot of you. What about the weavers?

BRUMMELL: *(Faintly.)* Can you see him?

AUSTIN: I see his coach.

BRUMMELL: The Royal coach?

AUSTIN: Is that real gold on the roof? That must have cost a bob or two. Tyrant! Enemy of Mankind! The Modern Anti-Christ! All the same, there's nothing quite like the show your English Royalty puts on, is there?

BRUMMELL walks towards the balcony as if his legs won't carry him all the way. The noise is getting louder and louder and now we can hear the jingling of horse brasses and the rumbling of carriage wheels. They have to raise their voices above the sound –

BRUMMELL: He'll come racing up the stairs –

AUSTIN: We just have a knack for it, don't we?

BRUMMELL: *'Beau!'* he'll say. *'Brummell!'*

AUSTIN: It's one of those things.

BRUMMELL: *'It's all forgiven.'*

AUSTIN: Like landscape painting and naval warfare.

BRUMMELL: *'Come back to court'.*

AUSTIN: You have it or you don't.

BRUMMELL: And I'll say –

AUSTIN: He's at the end of the street –

BRUMMELL: *'Ah, Wales'* –

AUSTIN: Fifty yards –

BRUMMELL: *' – there you are.'*

AUSTIN: Forty –

BRUMMELL: It was all a misunderstanding –

AUSTIN: Thirty –

BRUMMELL: A terrible mistake –

AUSTIN: Twenty –

Ten –

The noise is on top of them now – the frantic cheering, the thundering of the wheels on cobble stones, the jingling of horse brasses –

There he is –

BRUMMEL: Take the pistol –

The cheers and hoofbeats, drumming of carriage wheels and the military march are deafening. BRUMMELL steps onto the balcony. The noise rises to a crescendo. Carried away with enthusiasm, AUSTIN starts to bawl at the top of his lungs –

God save our gracious King

God save our noble King

God save the King –

BRUMMELL: The pistol – here –

He tries to push it into AUSTIN's hand but he's rigidly at attention, bellowing the anthem.

AUSTIN: *Send him victorious*

Happy and glorious

Long to reign over us –

BRUMMELL: Then I'll do it –

He jumps to the balcony, aims the pistol.

AUSTIN: What are you –?

BRUMMELL: *Princes, dregs of their dull race who flow through public scorn –*

What's the rest of it?

AUSTIN: Put that down.

BRUMMELL: You want him dead, don't you?

AUSTIN: In the name of suffering humanity and not a falling out between two worthless parasites. Give it here –

BRUMMELL: Too late. He turned the corner.

AUSTIN: Bugger off you fat bastard!

The sounds of the procession recede, getting fainter and fainter.

(Puzzled.)

He didn't stop. He's gone. Without stopping.

The bastard. The right bastard. Stopped not.

The sound of cheers and hoofbeats and carriage wheels disappears completely.

I did it.

(Realization.)

I said it. I said something witty. I came out with it, just like that –

Runs his tongue across his lips –

(Marvelling.)

You're right, there's a kind of metallic taste.

'Bugger off, you fat bastard'.

I didn't even know I was going to say it until I heard myself. It was like some force had taken me over, was saying it for me. I knew it was going to be good, I didn't know just how good. Out it came, just like that.

Turns to BRUMMELL who hasn't moved. He's staring in the direction of the departed carriage.

'Bugger' was a good start, got everybody's attention. *'Fat bastard'*, not bad, eh? And accurate. He's fat and he's a right bastard.

He looks closely at BRUMMELL.

Are you all right? You'll catch your death out there.

(He closes the window.)

He didn't look up once. Not once.

BRUMMEL: I first met him when I was at Eton, you know.

In the Meadow. We were fifteen or so. Everything lay in front of us. For him, a crown. For me, whatever fame I could command.

Closes his eyes, sways with longing –

To be young again. To have all that splendid journey still to make.

AUSTIN: He's forgotten you –

BRUMMELL: No –

AUSTIN: Yes.

BRUMMELL: Don't say that –

He grabs AUSTIN by the throat, shakes him –

It was Brummell who showed the English how to dress, who tamed their manners, if there was an Age of Elegance it was Brummell who led it, not that vulgarian voluptuary; it was Brummell, sir, *Brummell* who made poetry of Society.

AUSTIN: Let me go –

BRUMMELL: What was my reward? This. You.

AUSTIN: Get off –

BRUMMELL squeezes even more tightly –

BRUMMELL: What did he ever do? What will he be remembered for?

AUSTIN: It hurts –

BRUMMELL: What did he give the world?

AUSTIN: The Brighton Pavilion?

BRUMMELL: *(An outraged roar.) The Brighton bloody Pavilion?*

AUSTIN breaks free, goes on the attack as he gingerly checks his neck –

AUSTIN: You made yourself the center of attention of the whole world just by standing there, doing nothing more difficult or unusual than being yourself.

BRUMMELL: Who else could have carried off being me but me?

AUSTIN: You did nothing with your life but live it.

BRUMMELL: What else could I have done with it?

AUSTIN: Lived it in front of a looking glass with all the other buggers standing around watching you looking at yourself knowing they were watching you looking at yourself.

BRUMMELL: *(sharply.)* I always tried to look my best.

AUSTIN: The Modern Narcissus.

BRUMMELL: What?

AUSTIN: You know what happened to him, don't you? Fell in love with his own reflection.

BRUMMELL: I may have been the modern Narcissus but who did I hurt except myself?

AUSTIN: Well, who, when you get down to it, would a
Narcissist think was worth hurting except himself?

An anguished BRUMMELL holds the pistol against his own head.

BRUMMELL/AUSTIN: It was always, yes, ever in those things
that died the moment they sprang into life that I excelled –
which arts are more ephemeral than those of conversation,
wit and fashion? – but which, aha – which, you malicious
sprite – give us more pleasure in the long run of life?

*Choking with emotion, he turns to the cheval glass, smooths his hand
on the fabric of his jacket –*

BRUMMELL: To be spurned by the Mob – to be forgotten by
your King – poverty – exile –

His hand flutters as he tries to dismiss their importance –

They are shadows of a summers day. What are they against
this –

Staring with desperate longing into the glass –

This – daily *magnificence* of dress?

AUSTIN: So go on, then. Do it. Blow your head off. I'll get her
in again. *Death In Exile. The Dandy Done For.* Could shift
a few of those. Always a big seller, views of the corpse.
Especially with a moral behind them.

*BRUMMELL keeps staring into the mirror as AUSTIN picks up the
sack containing his possessions.*

AUSTIN: Me? I'll go back to England. London. No – Bath.
There's always something happening in Bath. The Royal
Crescent. The Assembly Rooms. The Theatre Royal. I'll
open a business – Austin – no – *'Auguste of Calais, Late Valet
to the very late Beau Brummell. Grooming Aids. Shaving Needs'.*

(He takes down a well worn overcoat and puts it on.)

I've emptied the bathwater, your shaving things are over
there, I think there's a little cheese left, I've cleaned out the
commode, there's half a candle, we're out of firewood –

He heads to the door –

Oh, the money to be made.

BRUMMELL: Suffering humanity? Revolution? The mail coach?

AUSTIN: The English had their chance at Waterloo when they could have turned their bayonets on their real oppressors instead of dying in their thousands for them. Bugger that. You going to do it, then?

He indicates the pistol still in BRUMMELL's hand.

BRUMMELL: You could hardly have missed.

AUSTIN: Then what? The guillotine?

BRUMMELL: What about the weavers?

AUSTIN: What about my neck? No thank you. A pistol to the head's a whole lot cleaner. It'll be over just like that. Or better be. I can get the mail coach to the boat if I leave now.

BRUMMELL takes the pistol from the side of his head.

No? I'd better have that then. The nuns wouldn't like it. I'll tell them you've had a bit of a let-down, take it easy on you.

He takes the pistol from him, heads to the door, digs deep into his pants and takes out a very large key on a piece of string. He pauses, as if daunted by having to actually leave.

BRUMMELL: That would be kind.

AUSTIN: It just couldn't go on like –

BRUMMELL: No.

AUSTIN: You do see that?

BRUMMELL: Yes.

AUSTIN: There's no future here for me.

BRUMMELL: I wouldn't wish to hold you back.

AUSTIN: Calais.

BRUMMELL: An awful place.

AUSTIN: Not to mention the wages I'm owed.

BRUMMELL: I see that.

AUSTIN: Bath.

BRUMMELL: Quite.

AUSTIN: The season.

BRUMMELL: I envy you.

AUSTIN: A little shop.

BRUMMELL: Excellent.

AUSTIN is still hesitating to leave –

AUSTIN: You wouldn't think of coming back? Ever?

BRUMMELL: Spoil an exit?

AUSTIN: I mean, just because he cocked a blind one to you-

BRUMMELL: Crawl back? On my knees?

AUSTIN: It's not that uncomfortable a position –

BRUMMELL: But hard to carry off with style.

AUSTIN: I suppose.

BRUMMELL: When one has nothing left, one does have that.

AUSTIN: Yes.

He turns the key in the lock, puts it back inside his pants again –

Right, I'm off.

BRUMMELL suddenly gives a cry of grief and anguish that brings him to his knees, as if the full weight of his humiliation and defeat has suddenly struck him –

BRUMMELL: Nooooooooooooooooooooo –

Using all his strength of will he pulls himself upright again, takes a shuddering breath and slowly expels it.

The coat –

He indicates for AUSTIN to head towards him, critically surveys how he's wearing the coat –

My first tailor, Schweitzer, was asked by a customer-

He tails off, tugs the coat into shape; stands back and gives an approving nod.

There.

AUSTIN: I never stole a penny from you. There's plenty would. Out there. Rob you blind. Sell your candle ends. Pinch your snuff.

BRUMMELL: Go.

AUSTIN: Did I steal one penny from you?

BRUMMELL: There's the door.

AUSTIN: There you are then.

73

BRUMMELL: Go.

AUSTIN spreads his arms –

AUSTIN: Oh yes? Oh yes?

BRUMMELL: The door?

AUSTIN: Check my pockets. Anything sewn in the lining? I don't think so. Clean as a whistle, me.

BRUMMELL: My grandfather – I told you he was in service? – left a room better than any man in England. When a thing was to be done, there he was. When it was done, he wasn't. It was a great gift. It made his fortune, he often said. You say you're going – you go. It keeps things simple.

AUSTIN: Right.

AUSTIN drops his arms. BRUMMELL indicates the cheval glass. AUSTIN hesitates, then checks himself in it.

BRUMMELL: Attitude.

AUSTIN: Attitude.

He straightens his back, heads towards the door –

BRUMMELL: That thing you said about Narcissus – who would he think was worth hurting –?

AUSTIN: Yes?

BRUMMELL: That was really very – you know –

AUSTIN: It was?

BRUMMELL: It might be the nearest you'll ever come to saying something worth repeating.

AUSTIN: You really think so?

BRUMMELL: You will excuse me? Today has been a little –

BRUMMELL steadies himself against the cheval glass and takes off his boots. He holds them out, inspects them, takes a pair of boot liners with screws, places them inside the boots and screws them to the correct size.

In dead silence he takes off his coat, inspects it, takes a brush and brushes it down, inspects it again folds it, hangs it carefully up.

He unbuttons his shirt, takes it off, folds it with great care, places tissue paper around it and puts it back on the shelf.

Finally, in the same silence, with the same practised, loving, professional hands, he removes his pants, inspects them at arms length, places them on a hanger and hangs them up.

This is more than a ritual for him, it's a sacrament. And he knows he may be doing it for the last time.

He starts looking for something on the floor.

AUSTIN: Beside the screen.

BRUMMELL finds his red velvet slippers and puts them on with a sigh of pleasure.

Without a word, AUSTIN sets down the sack, heads to the dressing gown, picks it up. BRUMMELL has spread his arms wide. AUSTIN slips it onto him.

Almost shyly, BRUMMELL asks him a question –

BRUMMELL: One last time?

AUSTIN nods. He goes to the door, clears his throat, opens it.

AUSTIN: The Duke of –

He hesitates. Starts again.

The Prince of Wales.

BRUMMELL draws himself up to his full height, all his cares dropping from his shoulders. He places his velvet night cap on his head, sits, with one elegant leg thrown over the other

AUSTIN picks up the sack, tugs the collar of the overcoat around him, heads to the door and exits. He closes the door behind him.

BRUMMELL: Ah, Wales –

Bright, intense, golden light floods in, bathing BRUMMELL with the radiance of Majesty; as he retreats into the ultimate privacy of madness...

THE END